Lepidoptera I:
Portraits Of My
Colorful Flying Friends.

A Coloring Book Celebrating Our Natural World

F. Scott Crawford

Lepidoptera I: Portraits Of My Colorful Flying Friends.

A Coloring Book Celebrating Our Natural World

F. Scott Crawford

Published by:

Black Rock Publishing
3661 Stockton Drive
Carrollton, Texas 75010

This is **Volume I** of my **"Lepidoptera"** coloring books. This volume presents several portraits of "Lepidoptera" (butterflies and moths) using line drawings which I digitally adapted from an astonishing series of scientific illustrations by Herman Strecker, published from 1872 through 1878. These images were reproduced from a set of the original documents, drawn and colored from life, for one of his subscribers. The set is now in the Smithsonian Library.

On the cover, the inside title page, and later in the coloring pages of this book, you will see an Old World Swallowtail photograph by Alex Staroseltsev; plus there is a Monarch butterfly photograph by Marco Uliana ~ Fotolia.com. These photographs are reproduced under license from Fotolia; I digitally traced them to make line drawings for you to color.

This coloring book provides two coloring pages for each guiding line illustration so you can color in the natural colors from the specimens and photographs, and then you also have an extra page so you can try your hand at whatever color combinations strike your fancy for each butterfly or moth in the series.

Produced in the United States of America.

ISBN-10: 1-51862-307-7

ISBN-13: 978-1518623073

DEDICATION:
For Maggie, "Forever & forever."

LET'S CELEBRATE YOUR OWN COLORFUL WORLD:

Use the colors that seem best to you.

"Stay in the lines" except when you have to go outside the lines to satisfy your artistic instincts and expand your horizons.

Relax. Concentrate. Use your feelings. Enjoy your creative impulses.

Lift your spirits. Take flight with your fantasy. Soar above it all.

Note: There are two pages for your colored drawings of each butterfly or moth in the series. This way, with the extra page you can first try your hand at natural colors ... and then do it again with whatever fantasy colors you like.

Herman Strecker Del.

2.

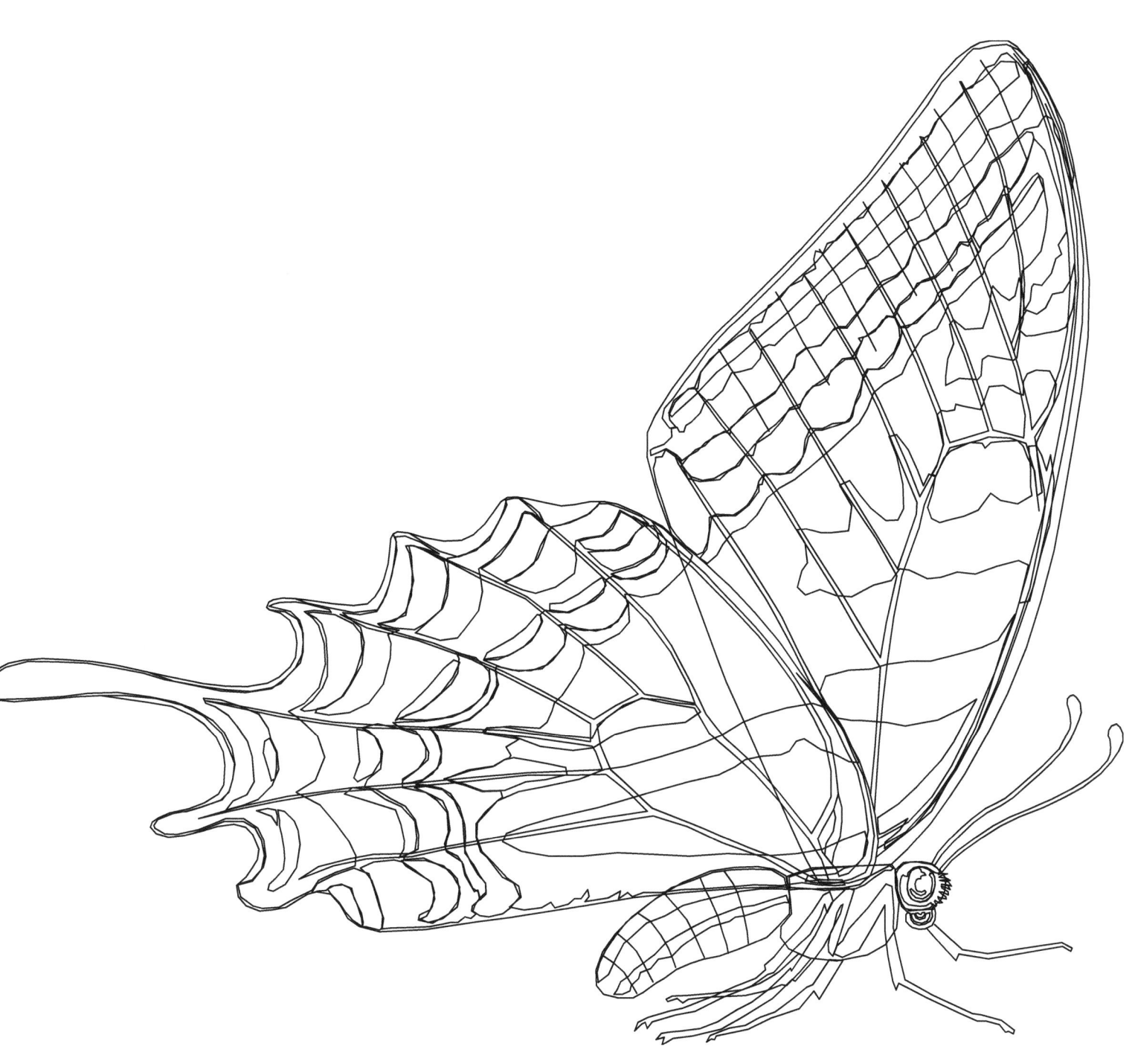

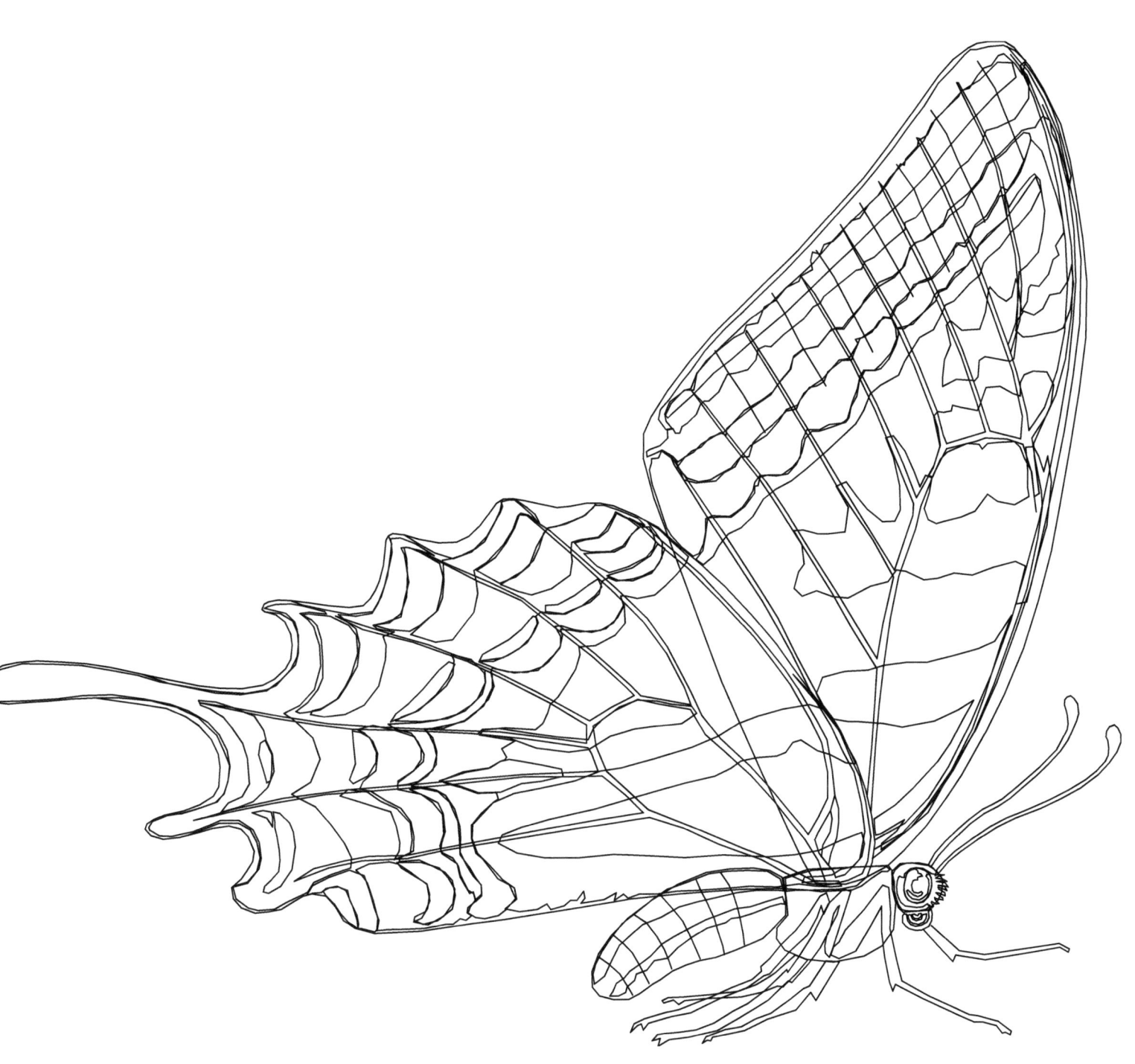

3.

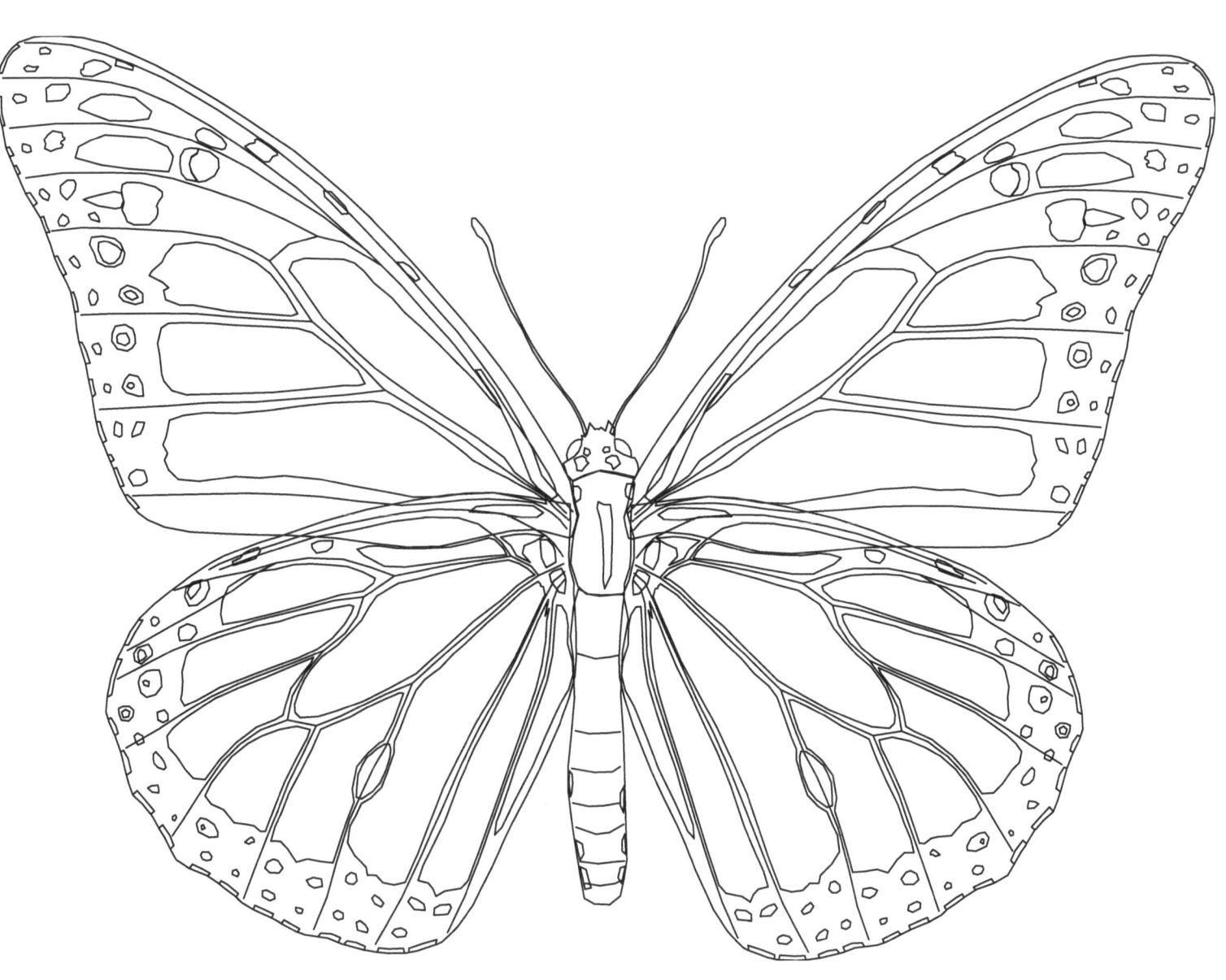